ULTIMATE GUIDE TO THE
PREMIER
LEAGUE
2021

Written by Rob Mason
Designed by Chris Dalrymple

A Pillar Box Red Publication

ISBN: 978-1-912456-68-0

PREMIER LEAGUE PLAYER OF THE YEAR

KEVIN DE BRUYNE - MANCHESTER CITY

Manchester City's marvellous midfielder Kevin de Bruyne was a deserving winner of the Premier League Player of the Year award for 2019/20. The brilliant Belgian international equalled the Premier League assists record by making 20 goals as well as scoring 13 times himself, with spectacular shots like his Premier League Goal of the month winners against Newcastle and Norwich in November and July.

Now 29 years of age, De Bruyne started his career in Belgium with Genk and first came to play in England with Chelsea. He was with the Stamford Bridge club for two years from January 2012 but only played in three Premier League games and nine in total. Moving on to Germany, he excelled with Werder Bremen and then Wolfsburg, before Manchester City paid £55m for him in the summer of 2015. In a league of superstars, he is arguably the greatest.

CONTENTS

The kick-off is the start of the game. Sounds pretty simple, doesn't it? But what you can do at kick-off has changed quite a bit over the years. Some people think some of the things you can do now in the Premier League have changed from the game's original laws, but in fact sometimes the changes in the laws means the Premier League has gone full circle and now does what was allowed right back when organised football started.

⚽ Since 2019, the team winning the toss has had the choice of kicking-off or choosing which end to attack in the first half.

⚽ From 1997 to 2018, the team who lost the toss kicked-off and the team who won the toss chose which way to kick.

⚽ The law from 2019 is the same as it was from 1873 to 1997: the captain who won the toss could choose ends or to kick-off.

⚽ In the very first ten years after football had laws from 1863 to 1873, it was the team who lost the toss who kicked-voff, with the choice of ends going to the team who won the toss.

⚽ In the beginning, there was no half-time, so if you chose ends, you had the advantage (such as the wind being in your favour) for the whole game.

⚽ From the 1880s to 2016, the ball had to be moved forward at kick-off. Since 2016, players have been able to start the game by kicking the ball into their own half, which is what they were also allowed to do before the 1880s.

⚽ When the FA Cup started in 1871, players who kicked-off could begin by dribbling with the ball. Since the mid-1870s, you have only been allowed to touch the ball once before someone else has to touch it.

⚽ Since 1997 you have been able to score with the first touch of the game. From 1875 to 1997, you were not allowed to do this, though it was permitted before then. No one is ever known to have done it with the first kick, although it has been done with the second touch.

⚽ Southampton's Shane Long scored the quickest ever Premier League goal. He scored in the eighth second of the Saints game against Watford at St. Mary's in April 2019.

6

PREMIER PUNDIT

Do you watch Premier League football and disagree with the former Premier League stars who are television pundits? Can you do better?

Where do you think the 20 teams in the Premier League will finish when the season is over?

Take a look at the Premier League table and work out where you think each club will finish.

Fill in the chart and see how well you have done by checking who finished where when the season is over.

If you think Liverpool will be top, write Liverpool next to number one. If you think Crystal Palace will be 10th, write them beside 10, and so on. When the season is over fill in the final positions and see how accurately you can predict the Premier League.

	My Prediction	Actual Result
Champions		
Runners-Up		
Third Place		
4th		
5th		
6th		
7th		
8th		
9th		
10th		
11th		
12th		
13th		
14th		
15th		
16th		
17th		
18th		
19th		
20th		

GOALS OF THE SEASON

The Premier League is famed all over the world for its great goals. These were the Premier League goals of the month from 2019/20. Which one is your favourite?

HARVEY BARNES

LEICESTER CITY - AUGUST
SCORED AGAINST SHEFFIELD UNITED

This Barnestormer of a goal was the winner for Leicester at Sheffield United. Barnes struck the ball as sweetly as it is possible to do so and, from just inside the box, it whistled into the United net.

MOUSSA DJENEPO

SOUTHAMPTON - SEPTEMBER
SCORED AGAINST SHEFFIELD UNITED

Strength and skill combined for Moussa Djenepo to hold off Ollie Norwood's attempts to foul him and still show tremendous two-footed talent to wrong-foot the Blades defence, create an opening and finish decisively.

MATTY LONGSTAFF

NEWCASTLE UNITED - OCTOBER
SCORED AGAINST MANCHESTER UNITED

With his brother Sean getting rave reviews, Matty Longstaff scored the only goal of the game on his Premier League debut to beat Manchester United. What a goal it was! Running on to a perfect lay back from Allan Saint-Maximin, teenager Matty struck an arrow of a low shot from the edge of the box that gave David de Gea no chance.

KEVIN DE BRUYNE

MANCHESTER CITY - NOVEMBER
SCORED AGAINST NEWCASTLE UNITED

The brilliant Belgian latched onto a Newcastle clearance, controlled the ball on his chest, let the ball bounce and then struck a perfect half-volley which looked even better as it smacked in off the bar.

SON HEUNG-MIN
TOTTENHAM HOTSPUR - DECEMBER
SCORED AGAINST BURNLEY

Spurs' South Korean star scored the kind of goal you dream about and normally can only score if you're really good at computer games. Picking up possession on the edge of his own box, Son ran the length of the pitch, outpacing the Burnley defence, before keeping his cool to shoot the ball home. Unsurprisingly, this unforgettable goal was named the Premier League Goal of the Season at the end of the campaign.

ALIREZA JOHANBAKHSH
BRIGHTON & HOVE ALBION - JANUARY
SCORED AGAINST CHELSEA

Johanbakhsh was a clear winner of the January Goal of the Month. His late equaliser against Chelsea on New Year's Day was as spectacular a bicycle kick as you could ever wish to see. Having also scored in his previous game, this is only of only two goals the £17m, Iran international has scored in 29 Premier League appearances for the Seagulls. What his goal-scoring lacks so far in quantity, he more than makes up for with quality.

MATEJ VYDRA
BURNLEY - FEBRUARY
SCORED AGAINST SOUTHAMPTON

Taking a long ball down on his chest with his back to goal, swivelling and wrong-footing two defenders as he took control of the ball, Matej Vydra then skipped past a third Saints defender before rifling home a fierce left-foot shot as he fell. It was a brilliantly taken goal for the Czech Republic striker who had come off the bench to become the match-winner.

BRUNO FERNANDES
MANCHESTER UNITED - JUNE
SCORED AGAINST BRIGHTON

As well as becoming the Premier League Player of the Month for June, he also scored the Goal of the Month. Fernandes' volley at Brighton finished off a slick move. Starting with a headed clearance from Harry Maguire, Nemanja Matic swept the ball wide to Marcus Rashford on the left. Rashford sped forward and then delivered a free dinner on a plate for Fernandes.

KEVIN DE BRUYNE
MANCHESTER CITY - JULY
SCORED AGAINST NORWICH CITY

Brilliant De Bruyne's second Goal of the Month came in a game where he equalled the Premier League's assists record for a season with 20 assists – and scored another goal for good measure. His Goal of the Month was City's second in a 5-0 win. Canaries defender Marco Stiepermann must have been dizzy trying to keep his eye on the ball as De Bruyne shifted it from foot to foot before curling his shot into the top corner from the edge of the box. Raheem Sterling led the applause that came from the players and staff in an empty stadium.

#PLAYERSTOGETHER

#PlayersTogether was the response of Premier League players to the coronavirus that caused so many deaths in Britain and around the world. Not only did Premier League football matches stop altogether for over three months, but when the league got started again, it did so without any fans being allowed into games. Football wasn't the only thing to close down. Just about everything else did too – including schools!

Liverpool captain Jordan Henderson came up with the idea of Premier League players giving some of their wages to help the brave people working in the National Health Service trying to keep everyone and their families as safe as they could. This project was called #PlayersTogether.

Harry Maguire, Mark Noble and Troy Deeney (captains of Manchester United, West Ham United and Watford respectively) joined Henderson as skippers to supervise the scheme. Setting up #PlayersTogether was complicated.

A lot of work went into it. Each club captain and their squads agreed to give a percentage of their monthly wage to the scheme. Players could donate more if they wished to. The footballers of the Premier League took control to do something positive to help when they could not play football.

> Jordan [Henderson] took the initiative to pitch the idea to the rest of the lads and it was a no-brainer for us. It's a great chance for players to show how much the NHS means to us - a cause that is close to a lot of players' hearts.

**Simon Francis,
AFC Bournemouth Captain**

> Jordan was brilliant in terms of setting up and taking the initiative and moving forward with it and then getting in contact with everybody. As soon as he did, everybody was on board straight away. So it's a brilliant, brilliant thing that he's set up and something that'll affect a lot of people

**Conor Coady,
Wolves Captain**

> As a group we just wanted to do something positive, and we feel we have taken a step towards achieving it. From the moment Jordan called me, the Premier League captains have worked tirelessly to ensure we could get #PlayersTogether in place in such a short time.

**Ben Mee,
Burnley Captain**

Former star England striker and Match of the Day presenter Gary Lineker said on Instagram:

"Absolutely brilliant. Well played to each and every one of them. Young men setting the right example. #Playerstogether "

**He then tweeted,
"Great job @JHenderson"**

LIVERPOOL'S TITLE

Liverpool were the worthiest of Premier League Champions. The Reds simply blew everyone else away as they strode to the title. So often they obliterated the opposition with early goals, but as Champions do, they also found a way to win when they didn't play so well.

At Sheffield United in September, Liverpool needed a costly slip from the Blades' on-loan Manchester United keeper Dean Henderson to win. He hadn't had a shot to save until he let Gini Wijnaldum's 70th minute effort slip through his fingers to gift Liverpool victory.

A few weeks later, Liverpool looked in trouble at another of the promoted clubs. With three minutes to play, the Reds trailed 1-0 to Aston Villa but still managed to win. That is the resolve that wins leagues. As Andy Robertson equalised in the 87th-minute there was no time for celebrations as Liverpool raced to restart. Their desire to win paid off when Sadio Mane came up with the winner four minutes into added time.

Their 100% record lasted until the ninth game of the season when a late Adam Lallana leveller earned a 1-1 draw at Manchester United. It wasn't until the end of February and the 28th game of the season that any more points were dropped. Liverpool

had an incredible 79 points out of a possible 81 before three second half goals by struggling Watford produced the most surprising result of the season as Liverpool lost 3-0.

Liverpool's high-pressing style saw them dominate almost every game they played. Defending from the front and winning the ball high up the pitch was their style. So many goals were created by superb wing-backs Trent Alexander-Arnold and Andy Robertson. Also, in the famous front three of Mo Salah, Sadio Mane and Roberto Firmino, Liverpool had sensational strikers ready to take advantage.

Defensively they were just as effective with Virgil van Dijk a towering presence in front of keeper Alisson while the whole unit was driven on by super skipper Jordan Henderson.

Liverpool had never won the Premier League title but have now joined Manchester United, Arsenal, Chelsea, Manchester City, Blackburn Rovers and Leicester City as the clubs who have been Premier League Champions. Looking at how good Liverpool are, any team wanting to take their crown will have to be both magnificent and consistent as the Reds aim to retain the title in 2021.

EARLIEST TITLE

Liverpool secured the Premier League title with seven games to spare. Manchester United in 2001 and Manchester City in 2018 previously held the record having wrapped up the Premier League title with five games to go.

HOME WINS

Liverpool became the first team to ever win every home game in a Premier League season. Chelsea and both Manchester clubs had previously managed to win 18 out of 19.

AWAY WINS

Dropping points only at Watford, Everton and Manchester United, Liverpool equalled Manchester City's 2017/18 record of winning 16 away games in a Premier League season.

RECORD POINTS

Liverpool smashed Manchester City's record of 100 points in a Premier League season. City set that record in 2017/18.

KLOPP THAT

When the season came to a sudden halt in March due to coronavirus Liverpool were miles ahead at the top of the table. At the time the Reds were 25 points clear of Manchester City and looked certain to win the Premier League for the first time. With the Premier League title all but mathematically secured Liverpool boss Jurgen Klopp won friends across the country by coming out and speaking with honesty and humanity. Speaking via his club website Klopp said, "First and foremost, all of us have to do whatever we can to protect one another. In society I mean. This should be the case all the time in life, but in this moment I think it matters more than ever. I've said before that football always seems the most important of the least important things. Today, football and football matches really aren't important at all. Of course, we don't want to play in front of an empty stadium and we don't want games or competitions suspended, but if doing so helps one individual stay healthy - just one - we do it no questions asked. If it's a choice between football and the good of the wider society, it's no contest. Really, it isn't."

Klopp continued, "I think in the present moment, with so many people around our city, the region, the country and the world facing anxiety and uncertainty, it would be entirely wrong to speak about anything other than advising people to follow expert advice and look after themselves and each other. The message from the team to our supporters is only about your well-being. Put your health first. Don't take any risk. Think about the vulnerable in our society and act where possible with compassion for them. Please look after yourselves and look out for each other."

Thankfully for Liverpool, the Premier League did resume after a 100 day gap and Klopp's side was able to get the handful of points they needed to wrap up the title.

It was a Premier League title that was well deserved and one that gained even more admiration from many football supporters because of Jurgen Klopp's unselfish and admirable comments in an awful situation.

PROJECT RESTART

Never before had the Premier League experienced such a gap as the 100-day break from mid-March until mid-June caused by coronavirus, which shut down much more than football. Schools, churches, pubs, other sports, theatres and most shops also closed down.

Sadly, tens of thousands of people lost their lives due to the pandemic. Doctors, nurses and frontline workers showed how extremely valuable they are by working bravely in incredibly difficult circumstances. With most people having to stay at home for several months the return of the Premier League gave everyone a boost. Football was back and it was a start of things beginning to get back to normal – even if it was the so-called "new normal".

Called Project Restart, the Premier League's resumption of top class football was very different to what the Premier League usually looks like and yet, in the circumstances, it was remarkably normal!

Supporters were not allowed into grounds so the stands were empty.

A total of around 300 people were allowed into stadiums including players, coaches, medical staff, match officials, TV and press people.

Nine substitutes could be named instead of seven and five could be used instead of three.

Drinks breaks were introduced in each half. Playing in the summer months made the conditions much hotter than normal. Every player had their own named drinks bottle.

When the Premier League restarted every team's shirts also sported a logo in honour of the NHS.

In the opening games, all of the players wore shirts with 'Black Lives Matter' above their number instead of their names. This showed support for equality for everyone. The opening games also saw all players and match officials 'taking the knee' in a further show of solidarity.

Teams did not come onto the pitch at the same time.

TV coverage gave the option of having artificial crowd noise so watching the games on television could sound normal, or at least like a video game. Viewers could also watch games without artificial crowd noise in which case games sounded like practise matches.

Changing rooms were extended to allow social distancing. If this was not possible other bigger rooms in the stadia were used for teams to get changed.

Every player, coach and member of clubs' medical staff entering grounds had to have their temperature checked on arrival.

Press interviews were carried out outside or by using Zoom to let journalists interview players.

To try and involve fans, grounds with big screens beamed live pictures of fans reactions at home onto their screens.

THREE AND OUT

The 2019/20 season was like no other. With every club having nine or ten games to play, the season came to a crashing halt due to the worldwide coronavirus pandemic.

Harvey Barnes and Jamie Vardy both scored two goals as Aston Villa were beaten at Leicester on Monday 9th March in the last Premier League match before what became known as the lockdown. Liverpool also had a Champions League match later the same week before all Premier League games were postponed.

No one knew when the Premier League would get going again – or if the season would even be finished. It seemed really harsh on Liverpool who, when the season was suspended, were a massive 25 points ahead of second placed Manchester City.

At the bottom of the table the situation was a lot tighter. Norwich were bottom, six points from safety but fighting hard to stay up. Four points above them Aston Villa were two points behind AFC Bournemouth, Watford and West Ham United but Villa had a game in hand. If they won it would lift them to 16th. With 29 points from as many games Brighton were also in danger.

There was certainly lots to play for (including the battle for European places) at the top, even if Liverpool had the Premier League crown all but mathematically sealed.

Eventually, 'Project Restart' saw Premier League players return to training (socially distanced, at first) and the season continued on Wednesday, June 17 after a 100-day gap! Having played in the last Premier League fixture before the unplanned break, Aston Villa got things going again by hosting Sheffield United with Manchester City playing Arsenal later the same evening.

To complete the season games had to be played with no crowds allowed in to watch but thankfully the world's most popular league could have all its games screened on TV. In 1939 things were even worse!

In 1939 the season was cancelled. This was long before the Premier League. Every team in the top flight had played three games but when World War Two began the decision was quickly taken to simply stop the season.

Eight clubs who were in the Premier League in 2019/20 were in the top flight in 1939/40. These were Arsenal, Aston Villa, Chelsea, Everton, Liverpool, Manchester United, Sheffield United and Wolves.

Sheffield United were the highest placed of these teams when the 1939/40 campaign was cancelled. Just like 2019/20, the Blades had just been promoted. They had won two and drawn one of their three games and were second in the table ahead of Arsenal, Liverpool and Everton (in that order). Manchester United and Chelsea were 10th and 11th with Aston Villa 14th and Wolves 16th. The top league had 22 teams then, two more than the Premier League has today.

Top of the league, with the only 100% record when the 1939/40 season was called off, were Blackpool. The Tangerines had beaten Wolves in their last game before the season ended. In fact most teams – but not all – kept playing but in regional leagues and cups.

The appearances made and goals scored by the footballers of 1939 did not count in official records. The Second World War was a terrible time for the world and lasted until 1945. After a season where only the FA Cup was played and regional leagues continued, the Football League got going again in 1946/47.

The same fixtures were kept as in 1939/40. Blackpool not only won the same three fixtures again, this time they won each one by two goals rather than the single goal they had won each one by in 1939. Blackpool finished the season in fifth place – with the champions being Liverpool.

BOXING CLEVER

Games on Boxing Day are often exciting. With crowds still in the Christmas spirit it is not unusual to get big score-lines. Liverpool and Tottenham in particular have enjoyed the last three Boxing Days. Liverpool have won 4-0, 4-0 and 5-0 the last three times they have played on December 26th, while Spurs have won 5-0, 5-2 and 2-1. It is not just Liverpool and Tottenham who have enjoyed the day after Christmas Day in recent years. Last season Manchester United beat Newcastle 4-1 while the year before Everton went to Burnley and won 5-1.

LEICESTER CITY 0-4 LIVERPOOL
26/12/19

LIVERPOOL 4-0 NEWCASTLE UTD
26/12/18

Roberto Firmino scored twice in each of these big wins over Leicester and Swansea with Trent Alexander-Arnold also getting on the score sheet in both these games. In each of the last two seasons Liverpool scored Boxing Day penalties, James Milner slotting home at Leicester with Mo Salah scoring against Newcastle who also saw Dejan Lovren, Xherdan Shaqiri and Fabinho find the back of their net. Brazil international Philippe Coutinho opened the scoring against Swansea with Alex Oxlade-Chamberlain completing the rout against the Swans.

LIVERPOOL 5-0 SWANSEA CITY
26/12/17

BURNLEY 1-5 EVERTON
26/12/18

Burnley didn't enjoy their Christmas Toffees as Everton raced into a 3-0 lead before the first half was even halfway through. Yerry Mina had the Merseysiders ahead in only the second minute, with Lucas Digne and Gylfi Sigurdsson adding to the lead. Although Ben Gibson pulled a goal back for the Clarets, Digne got his second goal with a screamer before Richarlison made it 5-1 in added time.

SPURS 2-1 BRIGHTON
26/12/19

Harry Kane scored in all these games against clubs from the south coast, taking the match-ball home to add to his Christmas presents in 2017 after scoring a hat-trick against Southampton. Dele Alli also scored. By the time Saints' Sofiane Boufal and Dusan Tadic also scored, they were already 4-0 down, with Son Heung-min having also found the net.

South Korea international Son went on to score twice in 2018's 5-0 over Bournemouth, where Christian Eriksen and Lucas Moura also scored before Kane struck.

In last season's game against Brighton, Kane and Alli scored again, with Kane making Spurs level after Adam Webster gave the Seagulls the lead, and Alli going on to hit the winner.

SPURS 5-0 AFC BOURNEMOUTH
6/12/18

SPURS 5-2 SOUTHAMPTON
26/12/17

MAN UNITED 4-1 NEWCASTLE UTD
26/12/19

Matty Longstaff raised Magpie hopes by opening the scoring at Old Trafford last year. Those hopes didn't last long, as two well-taken goals by Anthony Martial (either side of strikes by Mason Greenwood and Marcus Rashford) made it a handsome home win at the Theatre of Dreams.

TALK ABOUT TOMORROW

Premier League clubs all have top class academies but it is very hard for a young player to break into a Premier League team. Usually up and coming players go out on loan so you might find the best young players gaining experience in the championship or even on the continent. Here are eight stars of tomorrow to keep an eye on.

BUKAYO SAKA

ARSENAL
LEFT BACK OR LEFT WING

Date of Birth:
September 5, 2001

Birthplace:
Ealing, London

Age at Debut: 17 years, two months & 25 days v Vorskla Poltava, Europa League, November 29, 2018

Age at Premier League Debut: 17 years, three months & 28 days v Fulham, January 1, 2019

DID YOU KNOW: In all competitions Saka was in double figures for assists last season.

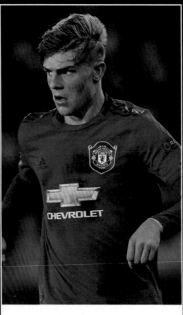

BRANDON WILLIAMS

MANCHESTER UNITED
LEFT BACK

Date of Birth:
September 3, 2000

Birthplace:
Manchester

Age at Debut: 19 years, one month & one day v Rochdale, League Cup, October 3, 2019

Age at Premier League Debut: 19 years, one month & 18 days v Liverpool, October 20, 2019

DID YOU KNOW: Williams scored his first Premier League goal against Sheffield United a month after his debut.

MASON GREENWOOD

MANCHESTER UNITED
STRIKER

Date of Birth:
October 1, 2001

Birthplace:
Bradford

Age at Debut: 17 years, five months & six days v PSG, Champions League, March 6, 2019

Age at Premier League Debut: 17 years, five months & ten days v Arsenal, March 10, 2019

DID YOU KNOW: Greenwood is United's youngest ever goal-scorer in European football – beating a record set by George Best.

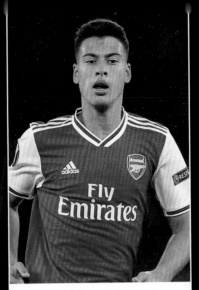

RHIAN BREWSTER

LIVERPOOL (on loan to SWANSEA CITY)

STRIKER

Date of Birth:
April 1, 2000

Birthplace:
Chadwell Heath

Age at Debut: 19 years, five months and 25 days v MK Dons, League Cup, September 25, 2019

Age at Premier League Debut: Yet to debut, but first on the bench as an unused sub at the age of 17 years and 23 days

DID YOU KNOW: Brewster won the Under 17 FIFA World Cup with England in India in 2017.

GABRIEL MARTINELLI

ARSENAL

STRIKER

Date of Birth:
June 18, 2001

Birthplace:
Guarulhos, Brazil

Age at Debut: 16 years, nine months & 0 days for Ituano in Brazil v Taboao da Serra, March 17, 2018

Age at Premier League Debut: 18 years, one month & 25 days v Newcastle United, August 11, 2019

DID YOU KNOW: Martinelli scored seven goals in his first seven games of last season and scored his first Premier League goal away to West Ham in December 2019.

REECE JAMES

CHELSEA

FULL BACK

Date of Birth:
December 8, 1999

Birthplace:
Redbridge

Age at Debut: 18 years, seven months & 28 days on loan to Wigan v Sheffield Wednesday, Championship, August 4, 2018

Age at Premier League Debut: 19 years, ten months & 12 days v Newcastle United, October 19, 2019

DID YOU KNOW: James was Wigan's Player of the Year when on loan there in 2018/19. He then scored on his Chelsea debut and went on to become the club's youngest Champions League scorer.

RYAN SESSEGNON

TOTTENHAM HOTSPUR

LEFT BACK OR LEFT WING

Date of Birth: May 18, 2000

Birthplace: Roehampton, London

Age at Debut: 16 years, two months and 23 days, for Fulham v Leyton Orient, League Cup, August 9, 2016

Age at Premier League Debut: 18 years, two months and 25 days v Crystal Palace, August 11, 2018

DID YOU KNOW: When Ryan scored for his first club Fulham against Cardiff City on August 20, 2016 he became the first player born in this century to score a goal in English league football. Exactly 26 months later his first Premier League goal was also scored against Cardiff.

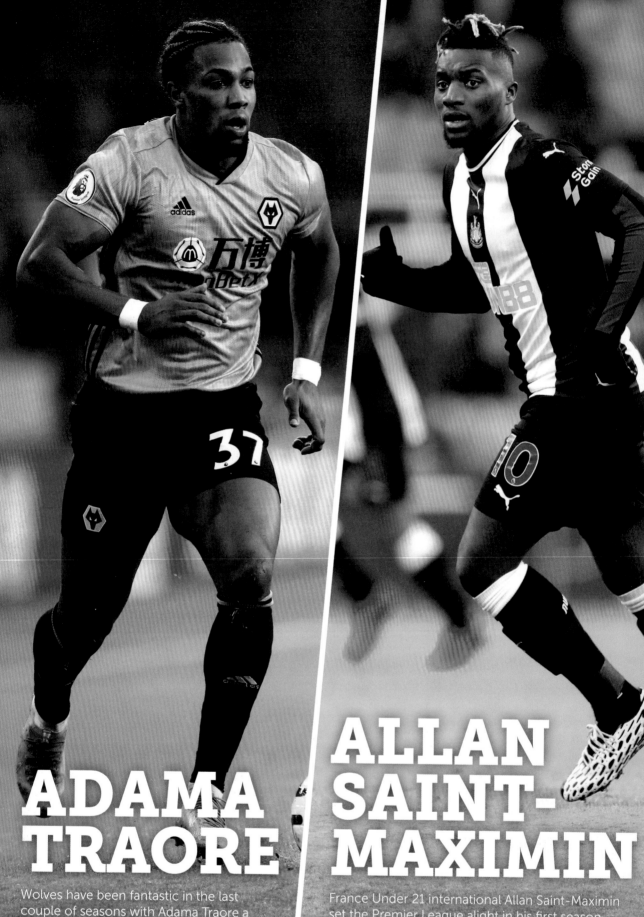

ADAMA TRAORE

Wolves have been fantastic in the last couple of seasons with Adama Traore a big part of their success. Always a winger of power and frightening pace Traore has added quality to his final ball. Now he is one of the most dangerous and difficult to defend against men around.

ALLAN SAINT-MAXIMIN

France Under 21 international Allan Saint-Maximin set the Premier League alight in his first season at Newcastle. A flair player who has the pace and desire to take people on, he is the kind of winger fans want to see get the ball. Still only 23 at the end of the season, Saint-Maximin looks set to be a big star in the Premier League.

SPOT THE DIFFERENCE

Can you spot the ten differences in this game between Everton and Newcastle United?

IT'S RAINING GOALS

On a wet Friday night in October, Leicester City equalled the Premier League record for victory with a stunning 9-0 win away to Southampton.

Ayoze Perez and Jamie Vardy both got hat-tricks with Ben Chilwell, Youri Tielemans and James Maddison also getting on the score-sheet on a night neither club's fans will ever forget.

Southampton were already trailing to a goal from defender Ben Chilwell when their own defender Ryan Bertrand was sent off in only the 12th minute. The Foxes showed no mercy. They were 5-0 up at half time and kept gunning for goals in the second half, the record equalling ninth coming from a last minute penalty.

FOR THE RECORD

- Leicester equalled the biggest ever Premier League win of 9-0, and became the first team to win by so many away from home.

- Southampton have been on the receiving end on the only two occasions a team have had two hat-trick scorers in the same Premier League game. Ayoze Perez and Jamie Vardy both scored three for Leicester, as did Jermaine Pennant and Robert Pires when Arsenal beat them 6-1 in 2003.

- Leicester equalled Manchester City's Premier League record of being 5-0 up at half time in an away game. City did so at Burnley in 2010.

- This was Southampton's worst ever defeat since joining the league.

- This was the biggest away win ever in the Premier League or Football League — the biggest since league football started 131 years earlier.

"We wanted to show we're a good side and we certainly did that"
- Brendan Rodgers, Leicester Manager

"The performance was a disaster"
- Ralph Hassenhuttl, Southampton Manager

VAR

VAR means Video Assistant Referee. This is where a key decision made by the match referee is checked by another official watching video replays of an incident. VAR is used for big decisions such as checking for serious foul play resulting in a red card, whether a foul was committed for a penalty, or if a goal should be disallowed because of a handball or for offside.

VAR was introduced into the Premier League for the first time in 2019/20. Can you remember any of these big VAR decisions from the first year of its use in the Premier League?

BURNLEY 1-2 ASTON VILLA

January 1, 2020

Jack Grealish's 'goal' was disallowed after it was initially given, and the ball was played on the centre-spot for the restart.

Teammate Wesley's heel was ruled to be offside during the build-up.

EVERTON 1-1 SPURS

November 3, 2019

Son Heung-min was initially shown a yellow card by referee Martin Atkinson after a tackle on Andre Gomes, but was then shown a red. Replays showed Gomes' injury was due to the way he landed rather than contact by the Spurs player, so Son's red card was overturned.

LEICESTER CITY 2-1 BURNLEY

October 19, 2019

Chris Wood thought he had scored an 82nd minute equaliser for the Clarets.

VAR disallowed the goal ruling Wood had tripped defender Jonny Evans.

ASTON VILLA 1-2 LIVERPOOL

November 2, 2019

Roberto Firmino thought he had equalised for Liverpool as Villa led 1-0.

VAR disallowed the 'goal' after judging Firmino's armpit to be offside.

DECISION - NO GOAL
FOUL
VAR

NORWICH 2-2 SPURS

December 28, 2019

Teemu Pukki thought he had put the Canaries 2-0 up.

VAR ruled the goal out for offside although some camera angles seemed to indicate he was onside.

SHEFFIELD UNITED 1-0 WEST HAM

January 10, 2020

West Ham's Robert Snodgrass thought he had managed a stoppage time equaliser.

VAR saw the ball had hit the arm of West Ham's Declan Rice in the build-up and disallowed the 'goal'.

CHECKING GOAL
POSSIBLE HANDBALL
VAR

HOW DID YOUR TEAM FARE WITH VAR?

This chart shows how teams benefitted from VAR decisions.

For example, +7 for Brighton means that overall, Brighton had seven more VAR decisions go in their favour than against. -6 for Sheffield United means that overall, Sheffield United had six key decisions go against them.

TEAM	VAR
BRIGHTON & MANCHESTER UTD	+7
CRYSTAL PALACE	+5
BURNLEY & NEWCASTLE	+3
LEICESTER, LIVERPOOL, MAN CITY, SOUTHAMPTON & SPURS	+1
BOURNEMOUTH	0
ARSENAL & WATFORD	-1
EVERTON	-2
ASTON VILLA & CHELSEA	-3
WEST HAM	-4
NORWICH & WOLVES	-5
SHEFFIELD UTD	-6

THEY USED TO DO WHAT?

Football is a simple game. That is one of the reasons it is the most popular game in the world. You can have a game with your friends whether there are two of you or dozens. Even if you've no one to play with, you can practise shooting against a wall or see if you can beat your keepie-uppie record.

While the basics of football are known and understood by everyone with an interest all over the world, the finer points of the laws of the game are always being changed. Whether this is a good thing or a bad thing is for you to think about and make up your own mind.

So, what has changed in recent years? These are just some of the changes from the last few years, plus a look back at some really strange old laws of football.

When a goal kick is taken the ball can now be played by a defender before it has left the penalty area. Before 2019/20 the ball had to leave the box before anyone but the person who had taken the goal kick could touch it.

When a defensive wall is set up attackers can not go within one metre of the wall. Before 2019/20 attackers could stand alongside or just in front of the wall if they wanted to.

Handball became much more complicated than it used to be! One of the main differences from 2019/20 is that now any goal scored or made involving an accidental handball is automatically disallowed.

Drop balls are now unchallenged. The referee drops the ball to a player from the last team to touch the ball before play was stopped – or to the goalkeeper if it is in the penalty area. Before 2019/20 one player from each team would contest a drop ball.

CHECKING PENALTY

HANDBALL

VAR

In 2019/20 the Premier League started to use VAR – Video Assistant Referees.

Looking back...

Over 100 years ago, way back before 1912, the goalkeeper could handle the ball anywhere inside their own half!

Back in the year 2000 the Premier League brought in a rule that if players argued with the referee, or kicked the ball away when a free kick was awarded, the referee had the power to move the free-kick 10 yards nearer to the goal. The rule was scrapped in 2005.

In the earliest days of football there was no crossbar and a goal could be scored no matter how high the shot was, so long as it went between the posts! Crossbars came into the game in 1875. The FA Cup had started in 1871/72.

Until 1992 the goalkeeper could pick up a back pass. The first year of the Premier League in 1992/93 saw goalkeepers not allowed to handle passes that had been kicked back to them.

Before 2013 there was no goal-line technology.

Before 1902 there were no penalty areas and before 1891 there were no penalty kicks. When penalty kicks were first introduced they were not called penalty kicks but the 'kick of death!'

If you could change one law in football, to make the game better what would it be?

The Premier League is watched and loved all over the world. Players from all over the planet come to England to prove themselves on the biggest stage. Manchester City's Sergio Aguero has long been one of the Premier League's biggest stars and now he has written his name in the record books as the highest scoring player from overseas in the history of the Premier League.

Twelve days into 2020 the Argentinian goal-machine overtook Arsenal legend Thierry Henry as the Premier League's top overseas hot-shot in style with a hat-trick against Aston Villa taking his total to 177 Premier League strikes.

Not only did Aguero overtake Henry as the Premier League's top foreign scorer, he also replaced Alan Shearer as the player with most Premier League hat-tricks – his threesome against Villa providing the 12th Premier League match-ball in the Aguero collection.

Not only did Aguero beat Henry's record, he did so in fewer games. The French striker scored 175 times in 258 Premier League matches for Arsenal. The Manchester City man swept past Henry's record with his 175th, 176th and 177th goals on his 255th Premier League appearance.

TOP SCORING PREMIER LEAGUE STRIKERS FROM OVERSEAS*

PLAYER	COUNTRY	TEAM	GOALS
Sergio Aguero	Argentina	Manchester City	177
Thierry Henry	France	Arsenal	175
Robin van Persie	Netherlands	Arsenal & Manchester Utd	144
Jimmy Floyd Hasselbaink	Netherlands	Leeds Utd, Chelsea, Middlesbrough, Charlton Athletic	127
Robbie Keane	Republic of Ireland	Coventry City, Leeds Utd, Spurs, Liverpool, West Ham, Aston Villa	126
Nicolas Anelka	France	Arsenal, Liverpool, Manchester City, Bolton Wanderers, Chelsea, West Brom	125
Dwight Yorke	Trinidad & Tobago	Aston Villa, Manchester Utd, Blackburn Rovers, Birmingham City, Sunderland	123

Thierry Henry

Robin van Persie

Jimmy Floyd Hasselbaink

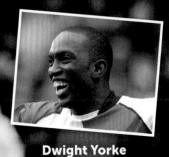

Dwight Yorke

Nicolas Anelka

Robbie Keane

*Up to the day Aguero broke the record.

THEIR BEST SEASON

Liverpool had their best-ever Premier League season but how well do you know the best season of every team in the Premier League 2020/21?

Arsenal

Arsenal have won the Premier League title three times but what made them invincible in 2003/04?

Aston Villa

Villa were runners up in the first season of the Premier League. When was that?

Bournemouth

The Cherries have once finished in the top half of the Premier League. Name the season they were 9th.

Brighton & Hove Albion

The Seagulls came into the Premier League for the first time in 2017/18. Which of their three seasons brought their highest finish of 15th?

Burnley

The Clarets best Premier League season came in 2017/18. What position did they finish in?

Chelsea

In 2004/05 Chelsea won more points than in any of their other four Premier League winning seasons. How many games did they lose that season?

Crystal Palace

Palace have finished in the top half of the Premier League season once. They did that in 2014/15. Did they finish 10th, 8th or 6th?

Everton

Everton qualified for the Champions League when they finished 4th in 2004/05. Who was their top scorer that season in the Premier League: Wayne Rooney, Tim Cahill or James Beattie?

Liverpool

Who was Liverpool's captain when they won the Premier League in 2020?

Leeds United

Leeds enjoyed their best Premier League season in 1999/2000. What position did they finish in?

Leicester City

In which season were Leicester Premier League Champions?

Manchester City

In which season did City achieve 100 points and score 106 goals?

Manchester United

United have won the Premier League a record 13 times. In 1993/94 they got their highest number of Premier League points. Was it 92, 94 or 96?

Newcastle United

In January 1996 Kevin Keegan's Newcastle were 12 points clear at the top of the table. What position did they finish?

Sheffield United

In which season did the Blades enjoy their best-ever season in the Premier League?

Southampton

The Saints' best season saw them finish 6th in a year when Sadio Mane was their joint top Premier League scorer. Name the season.

Tottenham Hotspur

Spurs were runners up in 2016/17. How many points were they behind Champions Chelsea: 1, 4 or 7?

Watford

Watford's highest Premier League placing of 11th came in which one of the last three seasons?

West Bromwich Albion

In the Baggies best season of 2012/13 which on loan top striker was their top scorer as Albion finished 8th?

West Ham United

Which Arsenal legend was top scorer for West Ham in their best-ever Premier League season of 1998/99?

Wolverhampton Wanderers

Wolves qualified for Europe in their best season in 2018/19. What position did they finish in?

(Answers on page 61)

PREMIER LEAGUE MAP

- NEWCASTLE UNITED
- BURNLEY
- LIVERPOOL
- EVERTON
- MANCHESTER CITY
- MANCHESTER UNITED
- SHEFFIELD UNITED
- WOLVES
- LEICESTER CITY
- NORWICH
- ASTON VILLA
- ARSENAL
- CHELSEA
- CRYSTAL PALACE
- TOTTENHAM HOTSPUR
- WEST HAM UNITED
- WATFORD
- SOUTHAMPTON
- AFC BOURNEMOUTH
- BRIGHTON & HOVE ALBION

NEWCASTLE UNITED

With Allan Saint-Maximin proving himself to be one of the most exciting and unpredictable players in the Premier League, Steve Bruce's well organised Newcastle made a mockery of those who doubted Bruce's tactical know-how. An early season win at Tottenham was the Magpies only victory in their first seven games. That run ended with a 5-0 thrashing at Leicester but they responded magnificently with 19-year old Matty Longstaff becoming Newcastle's youngest-ever Premier League goal-scoring debutant as he drove home a stunning winner against Manchester United. The result lifted the Tynesiders out of the bottom three in what was the gaffer's 400th Premier League game as a manager. That was the beginning of a sequence of six wins in ten that took United into the top ten at Christmas.

However just one win – against Chelsea – in the next ten dropped them to 13th before wins either side of the season suspension. Returning after lockdown with seven points from three games augured well, but just two points from the final six fixtures left the Magpies still perched in the same 13th place they were in before the hold-up.

FINAL POSITION:	13th
POSITION BEFORE SEASON SUSPENSION:	13th
TOP PREMIER LEAGUE SCORER:	Jonjo Shelvey (6)

QUIZ QUESTION: Who was the £40m striker who scored an early season winner at Spurs but didn't score another Premier League goal until June?

(Answer on page 61)

SHEFFIELD UNITED

FINAL POSITION:	9th
POSITION BEFORE SEASON SUSPENSION:	7th
TOP PREMIER LEAGUE SCORER:	Oli McBurnie & Lys Mousset (6)

Newly promoted, the Blades were the Premier League's surprise package. While other promoted clubs Norwich City and Aston Villa struggled, Chris Wilder's Sheffield side spent the season in the race for European places. What made this all the more remarkable is that just three seasons earlier United had been in League One.

With on loan Manchester United goalkeeper Dean Henderson in outstanding form the men from Bramall Lane were exceptionally hard to score against. Wins at Everton, Brighton and Crystal Palace and at home to Crystal Palace, Arsenal, Burnley, Aston Villa, West Ham and Norwich were built on hard won clean sheets before the lockdown. Once the Premier League resumed in June Sheffield started with another clean sheet in a draw at Aston Villa as they showed their lock-tight defence remained strong. It was at the other end that the Blades had difficulties. In the final section of the stadium they failed to score in five of their ten games. Losing their last three matches dropped United to ninth place but a top-half finish was a tremendous achievement.

QUIZ QUESTION:
The Blades drew with Manchester United in November but was it 0-0, 1-1, 2-2 or 3-3?

BURNLEY

Burnley were flying when the season suspension came. They had won four and drawn three of the seven games before the break. This run had begun with excellent wins over high-flying Leicester at home and Manchester United at Old Trafford. That was a vast improvement on a terrible run of four defeats at the turn of the year. This wasn't the first time the Clarets had experienced good and bad runs. After the October international break Sean Dyche's side had won three in a row, followed by two 3-0 wins and then three losses – the last two of those by 4-1 and 5-0. Another 5-0 loss greeted them at Manchester City on the resumption of the Premier League in June on a disastrous night for the club. However, a great run of four wins and three draws saw them earn a top half finish despite a final day home defeat.

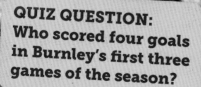

QUIZ QUESTION:
Who scored four goals in Burnley's first three games of the season?

FINAL POSITION:	10th
POSITION BEFORE SEASON SUSPENSION:	10th
TOP PREMIER LEAGUE SCORER:	Chris Wood (6)

(Answers on page 61)

MANCHESTER CITY

FINAL POSITION:	2nd
POSITION BEFORE SEASON SUSPENSION:	2nd
TOP PREMIER LEAGUE SCORER:	Raheem Sterling (20)

The defending champions often played brilliant football but just couldn't keep pace with Liverpool. Pep Guardiola's superstars frequently blew opponents away but occasional slip-ups resulted in them being unable to hang on to the Premier League crown. For instance, early season 4-0 and 8-0 victories over Brighton and Watford came either side of a 3-2 slip-up at newly promoted Norwich City, while in January after winning 6-1 at Aston Villa they were held at home by Crystal Palace.

With Sergio Aguero, Gabriel Jesus, Raheem Sterling, Kevin De Bruyne and Riyad Mahrez scoring regularly, Fernandinho as majestic as ever and Ederson incredible in goal, not least with his distribution, City were still to be feared. Missing the influence of the retired Vincent Kompany in defence, injury to stand out defender Aymeric Laporte at the end of August was a costly blow.

Liverpool looked unstoppable as they became champions in 2020 but City are determined to regain their crown in 2021.

QUIZ QUESTI
Who scored a
trick as City w
6-1 at Aston V

MANCHESTER UNITED

FINAL POSITION:	3rd
POSITION BEFORE SEASON SUSPENSION:	5th
TOP PREMIER LEAGUE SCORER:	Anthony Martial & Marcus Rashford (17)

United paid big money to strengthen their defence with the signings of Aaron Wan-Bissaka and Harry Maguire but it was the January buy of Bruno Fernandes that really excited the fans at Old Trafford. Player of the Year for the previous two years in Portugal (where he starred for Sporting Lisbon), he had created an amazing 239 chances in those seasons. Bruno quickly became the man to put the devil into the Red Devils attack. Winning the Premier League Player of the Month award in his first month in English football, Fernandes looks set to be a top star for years to come in the world's best league. With young striker Mason Greenwood also bursting onto the scene, Anthony Martial finding his best form and Marcus Rashford developing into an outstanding role model as well as an outstanding player, United finished the season strongly and will look to keep improving in 2020/21.

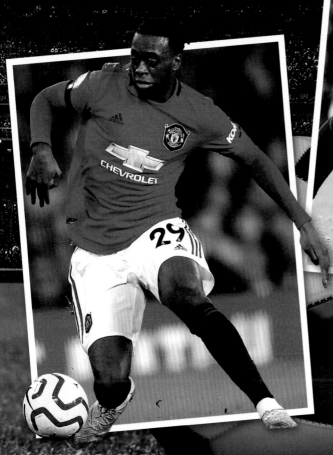

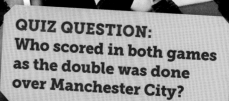

QUIZ QUESTION:
Who scored in both games as the double was done over Manchester City?

(Answers on page 61)

EVERTON

FINAL POSITION:	12th
POSITION BEFORE SEASON SUSPENSION:	12th
TOP PREMIER LEAGUE SCORER:	Dominic Calvert-Lewin & Richarlison (13)

A mixed season for the Toffees saw manager Marco Silva leave after a 5-2 loss in the local derby at Liverpool which left Everton in the bottom three. Former centre-forward Duncan Ferguson took over as caretaker boss and oversaw a great 3-1 win over Chelsea, a draw at Manchester United and another hard-won point against Arsenal before Everton gave their fans a Christmas present. That came with the appointment of Carlo Ancelotti, a top manager who won the Champions League with Real Madrid and league titles with AC Milan and PSG as well as the Premier League with Chelsea.

Ancelotti started his reign with back-to-back victories and by the time the season was suspended in March his only Premier League defeats had come at Manchester City, Arsenal and Chelsea. Following the league resumption seven points from three games showed promise, but just one win from the final six games left Everton with work to do to improve in 2020/21.

LIVERPOOL

The worthiest of Champions, winning the Premier League had taken an age for Liverpool but when they finally took the Premier League crown they did it in style. By the time the title was sealed with seven games to spare, the Reds had magnificently dropped a mere seven points, all of those away from home.

Throughout the team Liverpool simply did not have a weakness. Alisson in goal, Virgil van Dijk as a world class defender, brilliant wing backs in Trent Alexander-Arnold and Andy Robertson and the sensational front three of Sadio Mane, Roberto Firmino and Mo Salah were all brilliant. The man making them all tick was captain Jordan Henderson, a player underrated for so long but now increasingly appreciated as the ultimate team player. Henderson drove Jurgen Klopp's side on, always getting that bit extra out of the team. Hendo's influence was most obvious when he wasn't there. Liverpool's shock 3-0 defeat at Watford came when he wasn't playing.

Although the Premier League was secured after games were played behind closed doors without fans Liverpool had effectively been champions since even before the lockdown. They were that good!

FINAL POSITION:	1st
POSITION BEFORE SEASON SUSPENSION:	1st
TOP PREMIER LEAGUE SCORER:	Mohamed Salah (19)

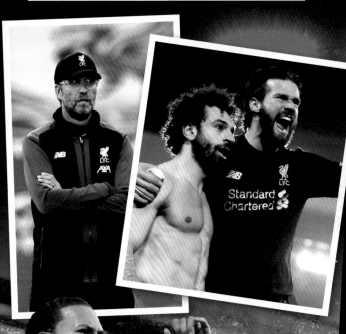

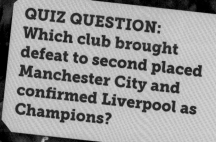

QUIZ QUESTION: Which club brought defeat to second placed Manchester City and confirmed Liverpool as Champions?

(Answers on page 61)

ASTON VILLA

FINAL POSITION:	17th
POSITION BEFORE SEASON SUSPENSION:	19th
TOP PREMIER LEAGUE SCORER:	Jack Grealish (8)

Newly promoted via the play-offs Villa found life back in the Premier League very tough despite a huge outlay in the transfer market. Well over £100m was spent in bringing in players. £32m was paid to Club Brugge for Wesley and Marvelous Nakamba, £20m was spent on Tyrone Mings from Bournemouth, £15m on Douglas Luiz from Manchester City, £12m on Ezri Konsa from Brentford, £11.5m on Matt Targett from Southampton and £9m on Bjorn Engels from Stade de Rheims. Over £8m was given to Kasimpasa for Trezeguet with another £8m to Burnley for Tom Heaton. With other players signed for undisclosed or lower fees, Villa just kept spending. They brought in five more players in January including £8.5m Mbwana Samatta from KRC Genk, ex-Liverpool goalkeeper Pepe Reina and former Leicester Premier League winner Danny Drinkwater on loan from AC Milan and Chelsea.

Although Villa reached the League Cup final where they lost to Manchester City, they found the step up to the Premier League to be hard going. Just seven games were won before the lockdown, two of those against strugglers Norwich who had come up with them. Things looked bleak when Villa took just two points from eight games, but eight points from the final four matches saw the League Cup finalists stay up with just a point to spare.

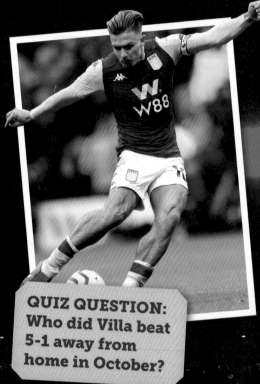

QUIZ QUESTION:
Who did Villa beat 5-1 away from home in October?

LEICESTER CITY

FINAL POSITION:	5th
POSITION BEFORE SEASON SUSPENSION:	3rd
TOP PREMIER LEAGUE SCORER:	Jamie Vardy (23)

Had it not been for Liverpool's truly exceptional season where they left everyone else trailing, Leicester City might well have been in another title race. Champions in 2016, for most of 2019/20 the Foxes were second or third in the table. Brendan Rodgers' side played some superb football and had the Premier League's top scorer in Jamie Vardy.

As always Kasper Schmeichel was one of the most reliable keepers in the country. In central defence Jonny Evans and Caglar Soyuncu were superb. Full-back Ben Chilwell was outstanding,

as was Ricardo Pereira. In midfield Harvey Barnes, James Maddison, Onyinye Ndidi and Youri Tielemans oozed class and inventiveness.

Newcastle were thrashed 5-0, Villa were beaten 4-1 and 4-0 and West Ham were overpowered 4-1, but most impressively Southampton were slaughtered 9-0 on their own St. Mary's pitch. The season break seemed to disrupt Leicester's rhythm. Just two games were won and four lost in the closing nine games as a Champions League place was narrowly missed out on.

QUIZ QUESTION:
Which one of these players did not score a hat-trick when Leicester won 9-0 at Southampton: James Maddison, Ayoze Perez or Jamie Vardy?

WOLVES

FINAL POSITION:	7th
POSITION BEFORE SEASON SUSPENSION:	6th
TOP PREMIER LEAGUE SCORER:	Raul Jimenez (17)

The midlands team with the Portuguese flavour continued to enhance the Premier League. Always attractive to watch, Nuno Espirito Santo's side had a cutting edge in Mexico international Raul Jimenez who they invested £30m in during the summer, after seeing what he was capable of having had him on loan.

Surprisingly Wolves didn't win until their seventh Premier League game of the season but after beating Watford they went to Manchester City and showed their quality by winning with two late goals from the pacey and powerful Adama Traore. The former Middlesbrough man was unstoppable throughout the season. Always a speed merchant to fear Traore improved his crossing and finishing to become one of the most improved players in the Premier League. Wolves won only three more points and scored just three more goals at Molineux than they did on their travels, so improved home would seem to be a big priority for 2020/21.

QUIZ QUESTION:
Who scored in both games as Wolves did a Premier League double over Manchester City?

(Answers on page 61)

WATFORD

Nigel Pearson's old school know-how was brought in by Watford in December after a disastrous start to the season had seen them part company with not one manager but two! However, Pearson was also dispensed with before the end of the season as the Hornets ended the campaign with Hayden Mullins in charge when they lost their place in the Premier League. Javi Gracia left in early September with Quique Sanchez Flores' second spell at the club lasting just three months. It brought just one win and an 8-0 defeat at Manchester City where they were five down within 18 minutes!

Taking over a team rooted to the foot of the table, six points shy of safety with 14 games gone, Pearson won four of his first eight games, with the only loss in that run coming at Liverpool. Amazingly when the all-conquering Reds came to Vicarage Road for the return fixture Watford stunned the champions-elect by ending their undefeated record with a 3-0 victory. Two great goals from Ismaila Sarr and one by the tremendous Troy Deeney made the whole football world wonder why Watford had been in trouble in the first place. That level of performance was not sustained as seven of the remaining 10 games were lost and Watford went down.

FINAL POSITION:	19th
POSITION BEFORE SEASON SUSPENSION:	17th
TOP PREMIER LEAGUE SCORER:	Troy Deeney (10)

QUIZ QUESTION: Watford famously inflicted the only defeat Liverpool suffered before securing the title. How many did Watford wallop the Champions by?

NORWICH

The Championship champions won a lot of friends but not enough points and slipped straight back out of the Premier League. The Canaries largely stuck with the team who had served them so well the previous season and will now look to bounce straight back to the Premier League, richer and wiser for the experience.

Being asked to face Liverpool, Manchester City and Chelsea in three of their first five games was a tall order. Beaten 4-1 at Anfield, Norwich impressed with their expansive attacking football but were too open at the back. It was a similar story as they lost 3-2 at home to Chelsea but they got their rewards as they sensationally beat Manchester City in another five-goal thriller after also beating Newcastle with a Teemu Pukki hat-trick.

FINAL POSITION:	20th
POSITION BEFORE SEASON SUSPENSION:	20th
TOP PREMIER LEAGUE SCORER:	Teemu Pukki (11)

Having beaten Newcastle six points from those first five games was a decent start but there would be just one more point from the next seven games as the goals dried up. A great win at Everton boosted hopes but it would be the solitary victory in a sequence of 17 games as the Canaries dropped further into trouble.

Ultimately, the longer the season went on the tougher the Canaries found it, but the club's strategy is to stick together and come back wiser, richer and stronger. Next time in the Premier League Norwich may well win more points as well as friends.

QUIZ QUESTIC
Who scored six goals in his firs five Premier Le games for Norw

(Answers on

ARSENAL

FINAL POSITION:	8th
POSITION BEFORE SEASON SUSPENSION:	9th
TOP PREMIER LEAGUE SCORER:	Pierre-Emerick Aubameyang (22)

Having had one manager for 22 years until 2018 with the great Arsene Wenger, Arsenal had three bosses before Christmas. After Unai Emery was sacked Freddie Ljungberg took charge for weeks until Mikel Arteta became the Gunners' gaffer. Under Arteta Arsenal started with two draws and a home loss to Chelsea but then didn't lose again in the Premier League until June after the season suspension.

Pierre-Emerick Aubameyang was the Premier League's joint top scorer in 2018/19 and once again Arsenal were heavily reliable on the former Borussia Dortmund striker. The new look Gunners showed they had no shortage of promising young talent with Bukayo Saka, Eddie Nketiah and Gabriel Martinelli making names for themselves. A final position of eighth was Arsenal's lowest in the Premier League since 1994/95 and Gunners fans will expect a significant improvement in 2020/21.

QUIZ QUESTION:
Who scored seven goals in his first seven Premier League games?

TOTTENHAM HOTSPUR

FINAL POSITION:	6th
POSITION BEFORE SEASON SUSPENSION:	10th
TOP PREMIER LEAGUE SCORER:	Harry Kane (18)

Like their North London neighbours Spurs swapped managers in the first half of the season. Fewer than six months after managing Tottenham in the Champions League final Mauricio Pochettino was replaced by Jose Mourinho. For the first full season at their super new stadium Spurs produced some mixed performances and results but with Harry Kane, Heung-min Son and Dele available, they always had plenty of flair players to thrill their fans although a hamstring injury to Kane on New Year's Day was a big blow.

Tottenham struggled to put a consistent run of results together. They didn't manage to go two Premier League games without defeat until November, with Dele and Son Heung-min getting amongst the goals as they drew twice and won twice. The same players were prominent again as Spurs won three in a row – including a big win over Manchester City after the turn of the year. A strong end to the season propelled Tottenham into the top six but it is the top four they will be aiming for in 2020/21.

QUIZ QUESTION:
Which South Korean player scored in the 5-0 win over Burnley when he ran with the ball from the edge of his own box to go on and score?

CRYSTAL PALACE

Palace played it quietly in the transfer market but grabbed a couple of cracking deals in bringing experienced defender Gary Cahill in on a free from Chelsea and striker Jordan Ayew from Swansea for a bargain £2.5m after he had been on loan. Ayew quickly got off the mark in a 2-1 win at Manchester United and then hit the winner against Aston Villa next time out before netting in all four games against West Ham and Arsenal as he showed a liking for London derbies. Just before the lockdown he then scored the winner in 1-0 wins over Brighton and Watford that lifted the Eagles into mid-table. When Palace returned to action with a comfortable win at struggling Bournemouth they were up to ninth, but a disappointing end to the season saw Roy Hodgson's men lose seven in a row before drawing with Spurs on the last day of the campaign.

FINAL POSITION:	14th
POSITION BEFORE SEASON SUSPENSION:	11th
TOP PREMIER LEAGUE SCORER:	Jordan Ayew (9)

QUIZ QUESTION:
Which Dutch defender scored the added time winner at Manchester United?

(Answers on page 61)

WEST HAM UNITED

FINAL POSITION:	16th
POSITION BEFORE SEASON SUSPENSION:	16th
TOP PREMIER LEAGUE SCORER:	Michail Antonio (10)

West Ham started with a 5-0 home defeat to defending champions Manchester City but won three and drew three of their next six games to climb to third in the Premier League table. A drop in form however led to manager Manuel Pellegrini losing his job and being replaced by David Moyes.

Under former Manchester United manager Moyes six games were lost and only two won in the ten games before the break caused by Covid-19 left the Hammers outside the bottom three only on goal difference. After the restart, back-to-back defeats had the Irons in trouble before a narrow win over Chelsea. They went on to take full advantage of games with doomed Norwich and Watford as those two victories from their final six games kept them in the Premier League.

QUIZ QUESTION:
Who was West Ham's manager in the first half of the season?

CHELSEA

With Super Frank Lampard back at the Bridge as manager the Blues began with a 4-0 thumping at Manchester United, lost on penalties to Liverpool in the European Super Cup and were held at home by Leicester before getting their show on the road with victory at newly promoted Norwich.

Big away wins at Wolves and Burnley brought hat-tricks for Tammy Abraham and Christian Pulisic with Abraham the first of four different scorers in between in a 4-1 win at Southampton. That was the second of a sequence of four successive Premier League victories but after that the Blues struggled to achieve back to back wins, not managing to do so until the games either side of the March to June shut-down. A strong end to the season provided a top four finish and with Abraham and Mason Mount two exceptional young English players, Chelsea remain one of the most exciting sides in the Premier League.

FINAL POSITION:	4th
POSITION BEFORE SEASON SUSPENSION:	4th
TOP PREMIER LEAGUE SCORER:	Tammy Abraham (15)

QUIZ QUESTION:
Who was Chelsea's first Premier League win of the season against?

(Answers on page 61)

49

SOUTHAMPTON

Losing 9-0 at home to Leicester City was not just a low point for the Saints season but for their entire history. To their credit Southampton held their nerve even after losing their next two games. Following defeat at home to Everton, Southampton were second bottom with just eight points from 12 games. Just one of those points came from their first six home fixtures as they made their fans suffer at St. Mary's.

FINAL POSITION:	11th
POSITION BEFORE SEASON SUSPENSION:	14th
TOP PREMIER LEAGUE SCORER:	Danny Ings (22)

Following a well-earned draw at Arsenal, sudden back-to-back home wins made the situation a lot better but their away form continued to be the Saints' strong point. Victories at Aston Villa, Crystal Palace, and most impressively at Chelsea and Leicester lifted them to be level on points with 10th placed Arsenal. The win at high flying Leicester would have been a stand-out result even without the revenge element after the 9-0 defeat in the reverse fixture, but to go to the Kingpower Stadium and turn the tables was a magnificent response.

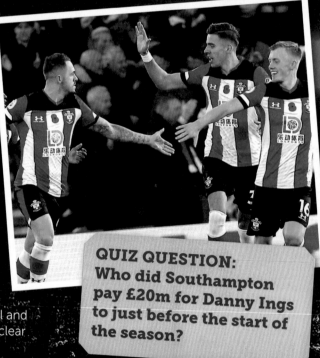

Danny Ings got the late win at Leicester, and was the Saints' main man throughout the campaign. He finished just one goal between Premier League top scorer Jamie Vardy. With only bottom of the pile Norwich losing more games at home and only the top two of Liverpool and Manchester City winning more away games, it is clear where the Saints need to improve.

QUIZ QUESTION:
Who did Southampton pay £20m for Danny Ings to just before the start of the season?

BRIGHTON & HOVE ALBION

Under new manager Graham Potter Brighton played some entertaining football and managed enough good results to largely stay out of trouble but without ever looking comfortable. Albion had to work exceptionally hard for every point they managed to win.

Highlights included doing the double over Arsenal while Spurs and Everton were beaten when they came to Brighton. With the consistent Matt Ryan in goal protected by Dan Burn, Lewis Dunk and Adam Webster, the Seagulls were difficult to play against, especially on their own patch.

Up front Neal Maupay provided the cutting edge and Brighton finally looked to have an alternative lead striker to the veteran Glenn Murray who was mainly kept in reserve to be used off the bench. Unbeaten away from home from January to the end of the season, and with the only defats in their last ten games coming at the hands of the sides who made up the top three, evidently Brighton were building a solid base to build on in 2020/21.

FINAL POSITION:	15th
POSITION BEFORE SEASON SUSPENSION:	15th
TOP PREMIER LEAGUE SCORER:	Neal Maupay (10)

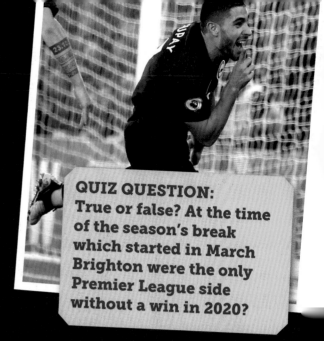

QUIZ QUESTION:
True or false? At the time of the season's break which started in March Brighton were the only Premier League side without a win in 2020?

AFC BOURNEMOUTH

Long term injuries to big summer signings Lloyd Kelly and Arnaut Danjuma didn't help Bournemouth's cause as the Cherries endured a difficult fifth season in the Premier League.

They actually made a good start. After winning at Southampton, Bournemouth were third after six games. Their next two victories were against Manchester United and Chelsea but the problem was these were Eddie Howe's side's only Premier League victories between that September win over Southampton and another south coast derby win in January, this time over Brighton.

FINAL POSITION:	18th
POSITION BEFORE SEASON SUSPENSION:	18th
TOP PREMIER LEAGUE SCORER:	Callum Wilson (8)

The Cherries were in the bottom three when the season was suspended despite their last two games seeing them hold Chelsea to a draw and only go down 2-1 at Liverpool where they had taken the lead through Callum Wilson. On that occasion they had to do without their other Wilson (Harry) as he was on loan from Liverpool. The two Wilsons were Bournemouth's biggest goal threat but ultimately they did not have quite enough to survive. The Cherries had done well to make their first foray into the Premier League for the last five seasons and will now be determined to return.

QUIZ QUESTION:
Which two players s in both the 3-1 win Southampton and t home win over Brig

(Answers or

WELCOME TO THE PREM
(NEWLY PROMOTED CLUBS)

New in the Premier League for 2020/21 are Leeds United, West Bromwich Albion and Fulham.

So, who are these clubs, what do they bring to the Premier League and have they been here before?

LEEDS UNITED
2019/20 Championship Champions

Last in the Premier League: 2003/04

Previous number of seasons in the Premier League: 12

Highest ever position in the Premier League: 3rd

Leeds were the last ever winners of the top-flight before the start of the Premier League. They were Premier League members for the first 12 years of the competition before being relegated in 2004. Just two years earlier Leeds had finished in the top five for the fifth year in a row.

After missing out in the play-offs in 2019, 2020 saw Leeds make no mistake as they won the Championship with Patrick Bamford their top scorer with 16 league goals. Players like Stuart Dallas, Pablo Hernandez, Jack Harrison, Helder Costa, Mat Klich and Ben White all had great seasons as they lifted Leeds back into the Premier League.

Without doubt their key man was not on the pitch but in the dug-out. Head coach Marcelo Bielsa has been manager of his own country, Argentina, as well as Chile. In the summer that Leeds dropped out of the Premier League Bielsa won the Gold Medal at the Olympics with Argentina. He also won league titles in Argentina and took Athletic Bilbao to the finals of the Europa League and Copa del Rey in 2012. It is not just Leeds fans who admire Bielsa. Pep Guardiola says Bielsa is, "absolutely at the top of the list as a manager."

QUIZ QUESTION:
What is the name of Leeds United's stadium?

WEST BROMWICH ALBION
2019/20 Championship Runners Up

Last in the Premier League: 2017/18

Previous number of seasons in the Premier League: 12

Highest ever position in the Premier League: 8th

West Brom are back in the Premier League after just two seasons away. When they left the big stage in 2018 the Baggies had enjoyed an eight-year run in the Premier League. Under former Croatia international and West Ham manager Slaven Bilic West Brom earned their place back in the big league.

Goalkeeper Sam Johnstone played every game, defender Semi Ajayi was outstanding and in midfield Romaine Sawyers and England international Jake Livermore have been dominant, but it was Brazilian Matheus Pereira who created most chances for Albion. The Brazilian is an accomplished technician who won 65% of the votes for the club's Player of the Year award. He was on loan from Sporting Lisbon during the promotion season and West Brom wasted no time in signing him permanently during the summer.

Sometimes Pereira is asked to operate out wide but Bilic likes his wingers to cut inside so Pereira remains a threat wherever he is asked to play.

FULHAM
2019/20 Championship Play-Off Winners

Last in the Premier League: 2018/19

Previous number of seasons in the Premier League: 14

Highest ever position in the Premier League: 7th

Play-off victors Fulham bounced back to the Premier League in even quicker time than West Brom. Scott Parker's side only dropped out of the Premier League in 2019 but beat Brentford 2-1 with two goals from left back Joe Bryan in the Play-off final.

Aleksandar Mitrovic scored 26 goals in 40 games for the Cottagers with midfielder Tom Cairney their second highest marksman with eight. With experienced players Tim Ream and Anthony Knockaert, along with promising young players such as Steven Sessegnon and goalkeeper Marek Rodak, the West London side came into the Premier League with the nucleus of a successful squad. Having worked hard to bounce straight back they will be determined to stay up and in 2020/21 they will hope to have learned the lessons of their previous time in the Premier League which lasted just a single season.

QUIZ QUESTION:
What is the name of West Brom's stadium?

QUIZ QUESTION:
What is the name of Fulham's stadium?

(Answers on page 61)

UNITED NATIONS

The Premier League is the most popular league in the world. Players come from countries from all over the globe. This is just a small selection of international players and where they hail from.

BELGIUM
Kevin De Bruyne — 1

GERMANY
Bernd Leno — 2

NETHERLANDS
Patrick van Aanholt — 3

REPUBLIC OF IRELAND Seamus Coleman — 4

SWITZERLAND
Granit Xhaka — 5

ITALY
Jorginho — 6

GREECE
Jose Holebas — 7

FRANCE
N'Golo Kante — 50

SPAIN
Adama Traore — 49

PORTUGAL
Bruno Fernandes — 48

USA
Christian Pulisic — 47

MEXICO
Raul Jimenez — 46

JAMAICA
Wes Morgan — 45

COLOMBIA
Yerry Mina — 44

BRAZIL
Roberto Firmino — 43

CHILE
Alexis Sanchez — 42

PARAGUAY
Miguel Almiron — 41

URUGUAY
Lucas Torreira — 40

ARGENTINA
Sergio Aguero — 39

GABON
Pierre-Emerick Aubameyang — 38

ZIMBABWE
Marvelous Nakamba — 37

GHANA
Christian Atsu — 36

IVORY COAST
Serge Aurier — 35

MALI
Yves Bissouma — 34

ICELAND
Gylfi Sigurdsson
8

NORWAY
Josh King
9

SWEDEN
Victor Lindelof
10

DENMARK
Kasper Schmeichel
11

FINLAND
Teemu Pukki
12

POLAND
Lukasz Fabianski
13

CROATIA
Dejan Lovren
14

SERBIA
Nemanja Matic
15

SLOVAKIA
Martin Dubravka
16

UKRAINE
Andriy Yarmolenko
17

CZECH REPUBLIC
Matej Vydra
18

JAPAN
Takumi Minamino
19

SOUTH KOREA
Son Heung-min
20

CHINA
Dong Fangzhuo
21

AUSTRALIA
Aaron Mooy
22

NEW ZEALAND
Chris Wood
23

IRAN
Alireza Jahanbakhsh
24

SENEGAL
Sadio Mane
25

GUINEA
Naby Keita
26

MOROCCO
Sofiane Boufal
33

ALGERIA
Riyad Mahrez
32

NIGERIA
Alex Iwobi
31

TANZANIA
Mbwana Samatta
30

TUNISIA
Yan Valery
29

TURKEY
Caglar Soyuncu
28

EGYPT
Mo Salah
27

17

28

24

27

21

20

19

22

23

30

37

TEST YOURSELF

How well do you know the 2019/20 Premier League season?

1) Who were the Premier League Champions?

2) Which team lost 9-0 at home?

3) How many players scored hat-tricks for Leicester in that game?

4) Who did Manchester City beat 8-0 in September?

5) Who scored seven goals in a three game spell for Chelsea early last season with two goals against Norwich, two against Sheffield United and then a hat-trick against Wolves?

5) Who scored alongside Christian Eriksen for Spurs when they drew 2-2 at Arsenal?

7) Who scored for Crystal Palace in away wins at Manchester United, West Ham, Brighton and Bournemouth?

8) Which club had the smallest stadium in the league?

9) What did Arsenal, Spurs, Everton, Watford and West Ham have in common in the first half of last season?

10) How many days gap was there in the season suspension between March and June?

11) Which team played in the last game before the suspension and the first game after it?

12) Which game resulted in Liverpool being confirmed as Premier League Champions?

13) During 2019/20 which player set a new Premier League record for scoring the most hat-tricks?

14) Which former Sheffield United forward scored in five out of six Premier League games for Everton early in 2020?

15) Which Italian club did Leicester sign Dennis Praet from: Roma, Sampdoria or Fiorentina?

16) Which Portuguese club did Manchester United sign Bruno Fernandes from: Porto, Benfica or Sporting Lisbon?

17) Which £40m recruit scored Newcastle's winner at Spurs in August but didn't get another Premier League goal until June?

18) Who was the Sheffield United goalkeeper who starred on loan from Manchester United?

19) The first two times Wolves scored more than once in the Premier League they lost both games. Everton and who else beat them?

20) 24 goals were scored in Norwich's first five home Premier League games. How many of those did the Canaries score: 2, 10 or 18?

HAT-TRICK HEROES ⚽⚽⚽

Scoring one goal in the Premier League is a noteworthy achievement. Netting a couple is tremendous but to score a hat-trick of three goals in one Premier League game makes you a hat-trick hero.

Which of these hat-tricks from 2019/20 is your favourite? There were 11 scored — with eight of them being scored by players playing away from home.

RAHEEM STERLING

West Ham v MAN CITY
SCORE: 0-5
DATE: August 10, 2019

Three clinical finishes, the first laid on by Kevin de Bruyne followed by two assists from Riyad Mahrez. Sterling's second goal was a delicate dink over keeper Lukasz Fabianski after a perfectly timed run.

TEEMU PUKKI

NORWICH CITY V Newcastle Utd
SCORE: 3-1
DATE: August 17, 2019

Three fine finishes from the Finland international, two with his right foot and one with his left. The first goal was the most spectacular as Teemu tormented Newcastle with a stunning volley.

TAMMY ABRAHAM

Wolves v CHELSEA
SCORE: 2-5
DATE: September 14, 2019

Tammy Abraham's first Chelsea hat-trick started with a swift turn and finish, continued with a text-book header from a pin-point Marcos Alonso cross and was completed with a brilliant goal that required strength, balance and terrific technique as he got the better of Conor Coady and fired home.

BERNARDO SILVA

MANCHESTER CITY v Watford
SCORE: 8-0
DATE: September 21, 2019

A close-range header and two six yard box left footers saw Bernado Silva claim the match ball on a day when Watford were blown away by City who were five up by half time.

AYOZE PEREZ AND JAMIE VARDY

Southampton v LEICESTER CITY
SCORE: 0-9
DATE: October 25, 2019

Two hat-tricks in the Premier League's joint record win saw Ayoze Perez score his first after a slick Foxes move, come in at the far post to half volley a Ben Chilwell cross into the roof of the net and complete his hat-trick with a great run to get on the end of a Harvey Barnes assist.

Jamie Vardy scored in the last minute of the first half and the final minute of added time at the end of the game with a penalty. In between he headed home another Chilwell centre on a night where the Saints couldn't wait to march in.

CHRISTIAN PULISIC

Burnley v CHELSEA
SCORE: 2-4
DATE: October 26, 2019

The perfect hat-trick involves scoring a header and a goal with each of your feet. A perfect hat-trick should also see you score your three goals without anyone scoring in between. Christian Pulisic achieved all this at Turf Moor.

SERGIO AGUERO

Aston Villa v MANCHESTER CITY
SCORE: 1-6
DATE: January 12, 2020

Power, poise and precision. City's all-time record scorer provided all three qualities in this brilliant hat-trick. Blasting the first from outside the box, the Argentinian then showed strength and desire to keep his balance and pick his spot for his second before completing his hat-trick as he burst through Villa's defence and had time to look up and fire home.

ANTHONY MARTIAL

MANCHESTER UNITED v Sheffield United
SCORE: 3-0
DATE: June 24, 2020

The first hat-trick in the Behind Closed Doors section of the season. Martial's clinical finishing was too sharp for the Blades. Two first time finishes from low crosses – one with each foot – preceded the hat-trick goal which came after a sublime 'give and go' with Marcus Rashford before a cute dink over the keeper.

Amazingly it was the first Premier League hat-trick by a Manchester United player since Robin van Persie scored three against Aston Villa in the game that sealed the Premier League title in 2013.

MICHAIL ANTONIO

Norwich City v WEST HAM UNITED
SCORE: 0 - 4
DATE: July 11, 2020

A hat-trick wasn't enough for Michail Antonio who scored all four goals in this game that confirmed Norwich's relegation. Two close range finishes and two headers - with two goals from set-pieces and two from open play - made Michail too hot to handle.

RAHEEM STERLING

Brighton & Hove Albion v MAN CITY
SCORE: 0-5
DATE: July 11, 2020

Raheem Sterling's hat-trick showed his appetite for goals. Persistence paid off as he refused to give up on a ball that kept trying to get away from him as he forced the ball over the line. Raheem had already scored with a cracker from outside the box and a close range header.

It was Sterling's second hat-trick of the season. Having scored the Premier League's first hat-trick of the season in August, this one in July meant Sterling also scored the last.

PREMIER LEAGUE RECORDS

Manchester United have won more Premier League titles than anyone else. The Old Trafford giants have won the Premier League 13 times.

97 points were not enough for Liverpool to win the Premier League title in 2018/19 but 75 were sufficient for Manchester United to take the Premier League crown in 1996/97.

No one defeated the Invincibles of Arsenal in the 2003/04 season.

Arsenal hold the Premier League record for the most games without defeat. The Gunners went 49 games without losing between May 7, 2003 and October 24, 2004.

Spurs went 32 games between May 9, 2018 and February 27, 2019 without drawing a match.

Derby County won just one Premier League game in the 2007/08 season. The Rams beat Newcastle United 1-0 in between 6-0 and 5-0 defeats at Liverpool and Arsenal.

Derby County (2007/08), Hull City (2009/10), Norwich City (2004/05), Wolves (2003/04) Coventry City (1999/2000) and Leeds United (1992/93) all went an entire season without winning a single away game

Manchester City have mega-firepower nowadays but in 2006/07 they only scored 10 goals at home all season. Only Huddersfield Town in 2018/19 have scored as few goals on their home soil.

Everton played in front of the lowest ever Premier League crowd. Just 3,039 saw their game away to Wimbledon in January 1993. At the time Wimbledon were playing their home games at Crystal Palace's Selhurst Park.

Gareth Barry has played 653 Premier League games, more than anyone else.

Between 2010 and 2019 Jordan Henderson played more Premier League games than anyone - 308.

Jamie Vardy scored in 11 consecutive Premier League games for Leicester City, between August 29 and November 28, 2015.

Jermain Defoe is the only player to have scored five goals in one half of a Premier League game. He did so as Spurs beat Wigan Athletic 9-1 in November 2009.

Sadio Mane scored a hat-trick in the space of two minutes and 56 seconds on May 16, 2015 when he was playing for Southampton against Aston Villa.

Alan Shearer scored 56 Premier League penalties - more than any other player.

Petr Cech is the only goalkeeper to keep over 200 Premier League clean sheets. He kept 202,

ANSWERS

SPOT THE DIFFERENCE from page 32

THEIR BEST SEASON
from page 32

Arsenal: They were unbeaten

Aston Villa: 1992/93

Bournemouth: 2016/17

Brighton: 2017/18 and 2019/20

Burnley: Seventh

Chelsea: One

Crystal Palace: Tenth

Everton: Tim Cahill

Fulham: Europa League

Liverpool: Jordan Henderson

Leeds United: Third

Leicester City: 2015/16

Manchester City: 2017/18

Manchester United: 92

Newcastle United: Second

Sheffield United: 2019/20

Southampton: 2015/16

Tottenham: Seven

Watford: 2018/19

West Bromwich Albion: Romelu Lukaku

West Ham United: Ian Wright

Wolverhampton Wanderers: Seventh

CLUB PAGES
from pages 35-53

Newcastle United (p. 35): Joelinton

Sheffield United (p. 36): 3-3

Burnley (p. 37): Ashley Barnes

Manchester City (p. 38): Sergio Aguero

Manchester United (p. 39): Anthony Martial

Everton (p. 40): Jordan Pickford

Liverpool (p. 41): Chelsea

Aston Villa (p. 42): Norwich City

Leicester City (p. 42/43): James Maddison

Wolverhampton Wanderers (p. 43): Adama Traore

Watford (p. 44): 3-0

Norwich City (p. 45): Teemu Pukki

Arsenal (p. 46): Pierre-Emerick Aubameyang

Tottenham Hotspur (p. 46): Son Heung-min

Crystal Palace (p. 47): Patrick van Aanholt

West Ham United (p. 48): Manuel Pellegrini

Chelsea (p. 49): Norwich City

Southampton (p. 50): Liverpool

Brighton (p. 50/51): True

Bournemouth (p. 51): Callum Wilson and Harry Wilson

Leeds United (p. 52): Elland Road

West Bromwich Albion (p. 53): The Hawthorns

Fulham (p. 53): Craven Cottage

TEST YOURSELF
from pages 56 & 57

1) Liverpool

2) Southampton

3) Two: Ayoze Perez and Jamie Vardy

4) Watford

5) Tammy Abraham

6) Harry Kane

7) Jordan Ayew

8) Bournemouth

9) They all made a change of manager. In Watford's case they did so twice.

10) 100

11) Aston Villa

12) Chelsea v Manchester City

13) Sergio Aguero

14) Dominc Calvert-Lewin

15) Sampdoria

16) Sporting Lisbon

17) Joelinton

18) Dean Henderson

19) Chelsea

20) Ten

Spurs' Son Heung-min scores his side's
third goal of the game against Burnley.
December 7, 2019